TEA
MAGIC

TEA
MAGIC

COZY SPELLS IN A CUP

CHLOÉ ZARKA GRINSNIR

STERLING ETHOS
New York

STERLING ETHOS
New York

STERLING ETHOS and the distinctive Sterling Ethos logo are registered trademarks of Sterling Publishing Co., Inc.

ISBN 978-1-4549-5557-3
ISBN 978-1-4549-5558-0 (e-book)

Library of Congress Control Number: 2024933112

For information about custom editions, special sales, and premium purchases, please contact specialsales@unionsquareandco.com.

Printed in China

2 4 6 8 10 9 7 5 3 1

unionsquareandco.com

Cover and interior design by Stacy Wakefield Forte
Cover and interior art by Chloé Zarka Grinsnir

To Mr. Fox,
for planting a
garden in which
I could grow.

CONTENTS

Introduction ρ. ix

INTRODUCTION

When tea becomes ritual, it takes its place at the heart of our ability to see greatness in small things. Where is beauty to be found? In great things that, like everything else, are doomed to die, or in small things that aspire to nothing, yet know how to set a jewel of infinity in a single moment.

—MURIEL BARBERY, *THE ELEGANCE OF THE HEDGEHOG*

There is *beauty* in the mundane, in the simple act of drinking vanilla tea during a cold winter evening or adding a little pinch of cinnamon to your hot chocolate, and feeling your home being wrapped in warm, comforting scents. There is poetry when you brew an iced tea on the hottest day of August and watch condensation create little transparent pearls on your glass, or when you bake the bread you have watched rise slowly on your windowsill.

That is witchcraft to me.

Witchcraft is stored in the little moments of life; it can be found in something as simple as a cup of tea. Waking up and stirring your morning Earl Grey can be your own little dose of magic, a peaceful pause before the day starts.

Witchcraft is all about intent and mindfulness. Nothing in life is trivial, and nothing is unimportant. Everything has a meaning. Lemon can cleanse negative energy, cinnamon symbolizes abundance, and simply putting a bay leaf in your wallet can attract money your way. All the little things that surround you already have magic in them.

I discovered witchcraft at a time when everything was changing in my life. I had just started working as a freelance illustrator while simultaneously moving to a new country, and suddenly everything felt new and strange. Witchcraft became a way for me to feel in control. It was the reminder that I had power, and I found great comfort in the notion that even little actions done with a lot of intent could impact my life positively.

One of the first spells I ever did was the simplest of things. After waking up and making myself a cup of coffee, I stirred it clockwise and focused on what I wanted to attract that day: peace, happiness, creativity. And just like that, with that simple motion, I was doing witchcraft.

Tea has always brought me a sense of comfort; it is a constant companion in my life. Even when I was a kid, there was the cup of tea with a splash of milk my mom had every morning. Then, there was often a cup of tea next to me, keeping me warm during sleepless nights when I was studying for art school. And the cup of tea my grandmother poured me after lunch, in her pretty china. Adding magic to my cups immediately felt like the most natural way to practice magic. I already had a mug on my desk, and suddenly, my steaming mug of chamomile was more than just that. It was also a manifestation of my own power.

so, what is tea witchcraft?

Many seemingly disparate crafts can cross paths and belong to multiple categories. Tea witchcraft is often seen as part of the more general practice of kitchen witchcraft, which centers around cooking and the act of making food to create spells and manifest things into your life. This book, however, will focus on tea alone.

Tea witchcraft has always felt like a such a powerful way to practice witchcraft to me. The act of preparing a cup and then drinking feels so potent, intimate, and palpable. Spellwork can seem abstract at times, but holding a cup of tea in your hands and feeling the warmth and enjoying the smell surrounding you is such a grounding moment of magic.

Just like with kitchen witchcraft, the power of tea magic exists in the ingredients and the choices you make when brewing your cup of tea. For that reason, this book will focus on the meanings and magical properties of various teas and all the ingredients you might add to your cup, like milk and honey. And to inspire and guide you in your practice, I will share some tea spell recipes you can try at home.

Tea witchcraft can also be part of the art of divination, as tasseomancy has been used as a way to see into the future for centuries. It is a divination method that consists in the reading of tea leaves, and while it is a complex practice, I will try to offer a brief introduction to it in the last part of the book.

I believe that tea witchcraft is perfect for beginners and seasoned witches alike. It is such a great way to start adding some witchcraft to your everyday life! With just a cup, anyone can create their own spells or simply boost their day with an extra touch of magic. Picking the right tea, stirring it, adding milk, or your own dried herbs . . . All these little actions are already witchcraft, as long as you do them mindfully.

I hope you will enjoy this little journey through the magic of tea!

TEA
(earl grey, oolong, matcha....)

TEAPOT
OR KETTLE
to prepare the tea

AN INFUSER
to steep the tea

A TEACUP
to drink your spell

the basics of
TEA WITCHERY

LET'S START WITH the basics. In this chapter, we will tackle all the tea witch's essentials and some tips and tricks for drying your own herbs. This advice is always adaptable to what you can or can't do. You don't *need* a collection of fancy teacups or your own homemade herbal tea to be a witch; it's fine to use your trusty old mug and a tea you've bought in the store. Remember that witchcraft is above all a personal path. This chapter is only here to give you ideas and inspire you.

the tea witch's essentials

Witchcraft should be accessible to everyone. There is no need to spend a lot of money to buy fancy new equipment: tea witchcraft is all about using what you can easily find in your kitchen. If you'd like a beautiful new teapot to brew your tea spells in, go for it! But this chapter isn't meant to urge you to buy everything new; it's simply a guide to help you assemble your tea witch tool kit. And in fact, you probably already have all these essentials at home.

Now, to start with the basics, you will of course need:

- ❖ **TEA**, obviously—black tea, green tea, herbal tea . . . any and all the teas! You can use teabags or loose leaves, whichever you prefer.

- ❖ **TEACUPS AND MUGS**

- ❖ **TEAPOTS**

Other useful tools include:

- ❧ **AN INFUSER**. There are many different kinds; you can even find novelty infusers. The basic ones are mesh tea infuser balls, tea-making spoons, and snap ball tea strainers.

- ❧ **A KETTLE**. Kettles make boiling water so much faster and easier! An electric kettle will be the faster option, but you can also get a cute stovetop kettle.

- ❧ All sorts of **FRUITS AND SPICES** to add to your tea. You can look at the correspondence chart in chapter 4 to find the different magical properties of these ingredients.

- ❧ And finally, some teas can be prepared with *specific tools*. For example, using a bamboo whisk to prepare matcha will enhance the flavor, and yerba mate tea is commonly brewed using a special gourd.

Tea witchcraft focuses heavily on the ritual of making a cup of tea. The way each step is performed and the ingredients that go into your tea can help you manifest your intentions and goals. The process of making your spells should first focus on your comfort and enjoyment. It's all about putting time and care into each spell. For that reason, you can add many other things to your tea witch arsenal: your favorite candles can help make you feel cozier, your warmest blanket can be a comforting addition, and even picking the perfect music to put on in the background can make a difference.

Your tea witch's essentials should be just like you. Everyone has different needs and different tastes, and there is never only one way to practice witchcraft. If you prefer colorful mugs with cute designs, then they should be part of your basics. If you're into fine china, then use that instead.

Think about the setting, too. If you're trying to drink a relaxing spell in the middle of a busy living room packed with other people, it probably won't work as well. On the other hand, drinking an energy spell while still lounging in bed won't be very productive, either. Adapt to what you're trying to manifest. Brew your sleeping spell in your most comfortable pajamas. Use your favorite tea set to prepare a self-love spell. Invent your own rituals, and make sure they work for you.

Every tea witch is unique, which means that your chosen basics will be unique too: you can be colorful, quirky, and creative; romantic and traditional, steeped in history; or whatever aesthetic and combination reflects your personality and fills you with positive energy.

how to dry your own herbs

While there is absolutely no obligation to dry your own herbs, it can be a meditative exercise, an opportunity to infuse some intention into your herbs. Much like kneading bread for fifteen minutes can be a time for mindfulness, preparing your own herbal tea can ground you more deeply in your practice.

Drying tea leaves is a complicated process, which means you almost certainly can't do it yourself. But you can absolutely dry your own herbs and flowers to make herbal tea at home. If you have an herb garden, you can harvest your own herbs. But even if you don't, worry not! A lot of herbs and flowers are easy to buy or forage, like mint, lavender, and dandelion. If you are foraging, just remember to be very careful and double check that you have picked the right plant and that they have not been treated with pesticides. Of course, you can buy potted herbs and start a little garden just for herbal tea. Or simply purchase cut herbs at the farmers market or grocery store. As always, this is about finding the method that works best for you. I'm living in an apartment in the middle of a city, and I can't exactly go foraging for plants. And while I would love to have my own herb garden, I'm afraid I've never been much of a green witch myself. But going to the store and picking herbs I like can be a little ritual in itself for me—it's a special moment I take out of my day. Find what *your* ritual looks like.

And now, to get into the heart of the subject, here's how to dry your herbs. The methods below work for both herbs and flowers, so you can easily adapt it to your needs.

TO AIR-DRY FRESH HERBS

It will take about 1 week for your herbs to air-dry.

If you live where it's humid or simply want to dry your herbs faster, you can oven-dry them. It's not the ideal way to dry herbs for tea, as it might slightly alter the taste. But it's still a very practical solution.

To oven-dry your herbs, spread them out on a baking sheet and set the oven at the lowest temperature possible, ideally no higher than 200°F. Usually, the leaves will need 1 hour to dry, but it's best to check every 15 minutes to make sure they don't burn. Flip the leaves after 30 minutes.

If you use an electric oven, you may keep the door slightly open so the air can circulate and prevent the herbs from burning. But do *not* open the door if you use a gas oven, as it could be a serious safety hazard!

Crumble the herbs once they are dry and store them in an airtight container. If you use a clear jar, it's best to keep it stored in the dark to preserve the savor of the herbs.

1 Brush off any dirt to clean the herbs. Generally, you want to avoid washing herbs when you can, so they don't mold, but if you have bought them at the store or foraged them outside, it's safer to wash them. Pat them dry very carefully after washing.

2 Make small bunches and tie the stems with some rope or rubber bands. Hang them upside down to dry in a warm, dry place with no direct sunlight.

3 You can also spread the herbs on some paper towels laid over a wire rack. Place the racks in a cool, dry spot.

OOLONG TEA
for wisdom

WHITE TEA
for protection

GREEN TEA
for mindfulness

EARL GREY
for abundance

correspondences
IN YOUR CUP

WITCHCRAFT IS ALL about ingredients and intent. Not every cup of tea needs to be magical, but when you want your cup to add a little bit of witchcraft to your life, use the lists in this chapter to guide your choices. They can be a good resource when you create your own tea spells, or simply help you manifest your desires.

Though there are several broad classifications of tea, there are many different varieties within those classifications. These lists are in no way exhaustive, but are simply a collection of the most known and consumed variety of teas. Hopefully, they will help you pick your teas more mindfully.

In the following pages, you will find a list of teas and tisanes and their magical properties and correspondences. While some teas and infusions can be good for health, this is not the focus here. These tea correspondences are here to help you pick a tea that best matches your magical intent.

tea correspondences

Teas all come from the same plant, called *Camellia sinensis*. Based on the type of leaf and the oxidation or preparation process, tea is classified into five main types: black, green, oolong, white, and pu-erh. Each main type has a host of different varieties, and this list also includes some of those.

Black Tea

Black tea is more oxidized than other tea, with a stronger flavor. High in caffeine, it's perfect for the morning. Black tea's magical properties can help with strength and energy, and they're very useful for repelling negativity. A great way to start the day!

Earl Grey Tea

Earl Grey is a black tea combined with bergamot, a type of citrus. And so, on top of the magic properties of black tea, Earl Grey also has the benefits of this fruit, which is likely a cultivar of lemon and bitter orange. Thanks to that, Earl Grey is a very good tea for manifesting attraction, prosperity, abundance, and love.

Masala Chai

Though chai is technically a black tea, its flavor profile and preparation differentiate it. Masala chai is brewed in milk and water, often flavored with a mix of spices called karha. Karha contains ginger and cardamom, but it can also have other spices as well, such as nutmeg or cloves. This tea has the advantage of combining both the magical properties of black tea and the spices in the karha: ginger promotes success, and cardamom helps with courage, clarity, and wisdom.

Darjeeling Tea

Darjeeling is from India, usually a black tea, and is categorized by how it is harvested. While Darjeeling is known for its distinctive delicate taste, its magical properties are similar to a regular black tea. So, similar to other sorts of black tea like Ceylon, Assam, or Lapsang, it can be used interchangeably in spells that call for black tea. Pick your favorite and enjoy!

Vanilla Tea

Vanilla tea is typically a black tea, though it can also be a rooibos (see the section on herbal tea correspondences). As a black tea, it will combine its magical properties with those of vanilla, making it a great tea for happiness, love, strength, and peace.

White Tea

White tea is made from younger or minimally processed tea leaves and has a lighter flavor. White tea's magical properties help with cleansing and protection, and it's a great tea for manifesting wisdom, happiness, and new beginnings.

Green Tea

The tea leaves used to make green tea are not as oxidated as the leaves of a black tea, which gives it a high level of antioxidants, vitamins, and minerals. Green tea's magical properties are great for healing and mindfulness. They can also help improve the mood and manifest new energies.

Matcha Tea

Matcha is a powdered green tea originating in Japan, usually consumed after being whisked into hot water. Over the centuries, an intricate ceremony has developed surrounding the consumption of matcha tea. Matcha, being a green tea, possesses all of its magical properties. But matcha also has its own added benefits, like promoting mental clarity and protection.

Jasmine Tea

Jasmine tea usually has a green tea base, but it can also have a white or black tea base. To better know the magical properties of your jasmine tea, consider the base of the jasmine tea you are drinking. Then add the strengths of the jasmine flower, which is great for love, attracting money, prophetic dreaming, aura cleansing, and confidence.

Oolong Tea

Oolong Tea is semioxidized and makes for a light golden or brown tea with a unique and delicate flavor. In witchcraft, oolong tea can be used to promote wisdom, deep connection, and focus, and thus it is a great tea to help with meditation and divination.

Pu-erh Tea

Pu-erh Tea is a special sort of tea originating from the Yunnan province of China, and it is known for its very earthy flavor. It is made from wild tea trees. It's a great tea for divination and psychic development and can also be used to manifest prosperity and wisdom. This tea may also be used in banishment spells.

fruit tea correspondences

Fruit tea is usually a mixture of tea leaves and fruits, though it can also be made of plants like rooibos or be a fruit-only infusion. And while you can buy fruit teas, they are also very easy to make at home. Simply add fresh fruit or a little bit of juice to your tea!

To understand the magical benefits of a fruit tea, the base of the tea must be taken into account in addition to the fruit's properties. For this list, however, I will focus on the magical properties of the fruits, as each fruit tea can have a different base. For fruit blends, you can combine the different properties of each fruit to determine their magical uses.

Apple Tea

A sweet gift of the harvest, the apple is often thought to be the most magical of fruits. Its ruling planet is Venus. In many cultures it was associated with the underworld (much like the pomegranate). Furthermore, when cut in half horizontally, the seeds form a pentagram. For that reason, apple teas can be great to use for divination. Apples are also a symbol of abundance, and their magical properties influence love, health, and creativity.

Peach Tea

Peaches are great for spirituality, and peach pits can actually be used to ward off negative energy. Because peaches are tied to the planet Venus, the magical properties of peach tea can also help with love and harmony.

Mango Tea

Mango is a symbol of joy, love, and luck. Because mango's ruling planets are both Mars and Venus, mango tea can help increase confidence and manifest personal power and success. It's a great tea to start the day or include in luck spells.

Orange Tea

Oranges are ruled by the sun and symbolize joy, health, and purification. Because oranges also represent success and growth, orange tea is great for confidence and career spells. It can also help increase creativity, which makes it a great choice for a morning tea.

Lemon Tea

Lemon is a potent purifier and is known for its ability to cleanse negative energy. This fruit is connected to the moon, and lemon tea is perfect for cleansing spells. Adding a slice of lemon to your tea is great for purification and protection.

Strawberry Tea

While strawberry tea is said to manifest happiness and luck, it's particularly known for its positive effects on both love and luck, as strawberry is another fruit ruled by Venus. You can even carry a strawberry leaf in your wallet for good luck!

Blueberry Tea

Known for calming the mind, blueberry tea is great to drink before meditation. It can also be used for happiness and luck spells. It's ruled by Venus, and its magical properties help with tranquility, peace, protection, and prosperity.

Cherry Tea

Also ruled by Venus, the cherry is a fruit with magical properties tied to the passionate side of love. Cherry tea is great not just for promoting love between people, but also for self-love and glamour spells. (Glamour spells are used to bring out your natural beauty and can help you feel more confident.) Cherries also symbolize abundance and prosperity.

Passion Fruit Tea

Passion fruit has calming properties, so this fruit can be used to help with sleep. It's a good tea to sip at night, and it can be used for sleeping and calming spells.

Pineapple Tea

Pineapple is ruled by fire and the sun, and this energy imbues the fruit with power and strength. It also promotes luck and prosperity, making it a good fruit tea to use in money and fortune spells. In Chinese culture, it is even a symbol of good fortune. Pineapple tea also symbolizes confidence and courage, as the sun energy in it encourages force, exuberance, and vigor.

Watermelon Tea

Watermelon's magical properties help to bring joy and peace. It's a great tea to drink if you want to release negative emotions. Watermelon is ruled by water and the moon, and it was an important fruit in ancient Egypt, as it provided hydration not only for the living but also for the dead crossing to the other world. Watermelon tea can also be used in love spells, as it is also a symbol of fertility.

herbal tea correspondences

Herbal teas are actually infusions, not tea, made with either one type of fresh or dried herb, or a blend of herbs. Because herbal teas do not contain tea, they don't contain caffeine, which makes them a great nighttime beverage. Herbal teas are perfect for sleeping or calming spells.

The magical properties of an herbal tea will depend on the plants used. If you are using a variety of plants, you may combine their respective magical properties. For that reason, be mindful of the blends you use.

Yerba Mate

Mate is made with a plant native to South Africa. Although not made from tea leaves, it contains caffeine. Mate is traditionally prepared in a hollow gourd by adding leaves and hot water. In witchcraft, yerba mate can be used to promote alertness, focus, and productivity. It's also very good for social energy and confidence.

Lavender Tea

Lavender is ruled by the planet Mercury. This fragrant herb repels negativity and deepens relaxation. It symbolizes peace, harmony, and clarity, so it's a great tea to drink before meditation or sleep, and you can use it for calming spells.

Chamomile Tea

Chamomile's magical properties are purifying and cleansing, and its ruler is the sun. In ancient Egypt, chamomile was even associated to the sun god, Ra. However, its ruling element is water, making it a very balanced and harmonious magical ingredient. Chamomile is an ancient healing herbs that is known for its ability to undo hexes and curses. It can even attract luck. Chamomile tea is great before bed as it's very relaxing, and it can also be used for protection spells.

Peppermint Tea

Peppermint tea not only is great for helping relieve nausea and stomachaches; it also has purifying and healing magical properties. It promotes cleansing, protection, and clarity. Traditionally, it has even been used to help with the grieving process. It can be used in protection and prosperity spells. Peppermint is ruled by Mercury, a planet whose energy is known for helping with meditation.

Rooibos Tea

Rooibos tea is a particular type of herbal tea, sometimes called red tea, and while its taste is similar to a black tea, it's notably caffeine-free. Rooibos tea is great for courage, determination, and strength. You can use it in spells to boost your confidence.

Ginger Tea

Ginger tea's magical properties can help you let go of anger and frustration. Ginger is ruled by Mars and promotes success and prosperity, too, so it's a great tea to use for a career or a money spell.

Dandelion Tea

Dandelion tea is grounding, healing, and purifying. It can help with divination as it will enhance psychic abilities. Dandelions are ruled by Jupiter. They're a symbol of abundance and good luck—after all, dandelion flowers have always been tied to wish making. It's a powerful magical ingredient, so use dandelion tea in any spell to give it a magic boost.

Ginseng Tea

Ginseng is ruled by Saturn and Uranus. It is known for its revitalizing properties, but it can also promote passion and success. Ginseng tea is great for love spells, money spells, and even career spells. It's also good for protection and energy.

Hibiscus Tea

Hibiscus, a tropical flower used to brew a delicious and bracing sour tea, is ruled by Venus and symbolizes love. It can be great a choice for self-love spells as it promotes acceptance and sensitivity. It's also a good tea to drink for cleansing and protection.

Lemon Balm Tea

Tea made from lemon balm can help relieve anxiety. It's ruled by Neptune and the moon. Its magical properties are happiness, success, love, and healing, which makes it a great addition to love and career spells.

Sage Tea

Sage is ruled by Jupiter. Sage tea can help you ground yourself, and because of that, it is a good tea to use for meditation or calming spells. It also has protective and cleansing properties. Sage symbolizes wisdom and purification.

Verbena Tea

Verbena tea is great for helping you break bad habits. Its magical properties can assist with protection, inspiration, and tranquility. Because it's ruled by Venus, verbena also promotes abundance and love. It's great for cleansing spells as it is known for banishing negative energy.

Spearmint Tea

Mint is ruled by Mercury and symbolizes joy and success. Mint tea encourages new beginnings and helps with decision-making. It also promotes abundance, prosperity, and healing.

Rosemary Tea

Rosemary is ruled by the sun, and its tea is good for memory and concentration. It also helps with repelling nightmares and is a good tea to add to any cleansing spells, as it removes negative energies.

Thyme Tea

Thyme is ruled by Venus, and its magical properties help with courage, strength, purification, and healing. Thyme tea promotes a peaceful sleep and is good for prosperity and luck spells, too.

Nettle Tea

Nettle tea is protective and repels negative energy. Its magical properties promote well-being and healing, and can help with strength and warding spells. Its plant, nettle, can sting when touched, which makes it a perfect plant for protection as it even knows how to protect itself. Nettle is ruled by Mars and yet is known as a very nurturing plant.

Cinnamon Tea

Cinnamon is ruled by Mercury and the sun. This tea can be very protective and is often used to banish negative energies, but it can also bring you luck, which makes it a great addition to spells relating to success and fortune. It's also a great tea for healing spells.

Fennel Tea

Fennel is ruled by Mercury. Its magical properties promote healing, release, courage, and confidence. It's a great tea for protection spells, but can also help with meditation and divination. It repels negative energy.

milk, sugar, syrup, AND SPICE

NOW THAT YOU know everything about the magical properties of tea, you can start adding other ingredients to your cup. Witchcraft doesn't need to be expensive or complicated to be effective. In fact, there are many easy and accessible ways to add magic to your tea.

Do you take your tea with milk and honey? A slice of lemon, maybe? All of these additions have their own magic. When creating a tea spell, they can be added for an extra boost of intent, carrying with them their respective energetic correspondences.

the magical properties of milk

Milk is a delicious addition to tea—and it can add an extra touch of witchcraft. There are different varieties of milk, and they all have their own magical properties. This section will describe the properties of both dairy and nondairy milk, so you can use it in your tea magic spellwork, regardless of dietary choices or restrictions.

It's most common to brew tea leaves in water, but you can also directly brew your tea with milk. Masala chai is most often made this way, and this technique can be used with a lot of other teas and herbal teas. Brewing tea by using this method will make the magical properties of milk more potent in your spell, not to mention that it makes for a comforting and delicious beverage. Try different combinations to find ones you enjoy. I personally love to infuse lavender tea in milk—the delicate floral taste of the lavender works so well with a milky base, and lavender is excellent for promoting healing and calming energy.

Cow's Milk

This is the milk you are perhaps the most familiar with. Cow's milk is known for helping with prosperity and abundance—it's a very nurturing milk that is great for protection spells too. (You can use lactose-free milk if needed; it will not affect the spell.) Cow's milk is very versatile and tastes great with most teas. Feel free to use whole milk or skim to your liking, as it won't impact its magical properties. You can usually swap any milk for cow's milk in a spell.

Goat's Milk

In many different cultures and mythologies, goats are associated with magic, determination, abundance, and good luck. Goat's milk has a stronger taste than cow's milk. It helps with power and success, and it can be a powerful addition for career spells. It tastes great with black tea and enhances its magical properties.

Soy Milk

Soy milk is an easy plant-based option. A splash of soy milk will promote success, protect against negativity, and help you get more in touch with your intuition. It's a versatile addition to your cup: you can use it for both career and protection spells, or even to increase the accuracy of divination. For that reason, you can drink it during a tarot reading or whenever you are practicing divination.

Coconut Milk

Coconut milk has a rich, luxurious taste, which can be lovely with a variety of flavors. I like it with matcha—the magical correspondences of this tea with coconut milk go hand in hand, as they both have protective properties. And while matcha helps with mental clarity, coconut milk promotes intuition and cleansing.

Oat Milk

Oat milk has a fairly neutral taste, so it pairs well with most teas. It is also strongly grounding, which can be helpful before a meditation. Grounding is essential to any spellwork, so oat milk is good to drink before practicing witchcraft in general. Its magical properties also help with prosperity and healing.

Rice Milk

Rice milk's taste is on the sweeter side, but it works well with most flavors of teas. Rice promotes abundance, blessings, feelings of security, and protection. Rice milk is a good addition to fortune, cleansing, and blessing spells.

Hazelnut Milk

Hazelnut milk is very sweet and rich in taste. It promotes luck and helps with accessing wisdom, having prophetic or inspiring dreams, and doing accurate and inspiring divinatory readings. Drink it before bed with a calming herbal tea like lavender to enhance its magical properties.

Almond Milk

Almond milk has many magical proprieties. It's healing and effective in helping with prosperity, abundance, and luck, and thus is a great milk to help with new goals and new chapters of your life.

magical additions

Your pantry is already full of ingredients with magical properties—everything in this world has them, and their effects can be felt in powerful ways when they are used with intent. Using different ingredients to create a potion, spell, or ritual is a foundational practice in tea witchcraft (and kitchen witchcraft in general). So while it may not seem like adding some honey or spices to your tea will have a big impact, these ingredients can, in fact, strengthen a spell or add new dimensions to its effects. Below you will find a list of different ingredients you might consider adding to your tea, along with their magical properties. Although this list is not exhaustive, it will give you an idea of the multidimensional properties of even the most common additions to your cup of tea.

You can use all the spices in this list whole or ground into powder. A spice's physical form won't alter its magical properties.

Honey

Honeybees were sacred in many ancient civilizations, such as Greece and Egypt, and honey was often seen as a sacred substance. It was even used as part of the mummification process in ancient Egypt. It's good for health and a potent magical ingredient with many uses. Adding a spoonful of honey to your tea is great for promoting happiness and courage. Honey's magical properties also help with love, healing, prosperity, and passion.

Brown Sugar

In magic, sugar draws things your way. Unlike salt, which is used to repel, sugar attracts. You can absolutely use white sugar to sweeten both your tea and your spells, but brown sugar is richer in flavor and packs in different magical abilities. Where regular sugar mostly attracts love, brown sugar also attracts comfort, healing, and friendship.

Vanilla Extract

Vanilla extract is a tasty and easy way to add the magical properties of love, self-love, and happiness to your tea. It is known as a love spice because it is highly physical and effective in seduction. This doesn't have to relate only to romantic attraction, as it can also attract friends your way. Its warm and down-to-earth magical properties also help with comfort and inner peace. You can swap vanilla extract for vanilla beans if you have some in your pantry; it won't alter its magical effects.

Maple Syrup

Maple syrup is a tasty way to sweeten your tea. In many different folklore traditions, maple trees are associated with strength, protection, prosperity, and the resilience of nature. As a direct by-product of these trees, maple syrup carries much of the same magical properties.

Lemon (Sliced or as Juice)

Lemon is a powerful purifier, whether incorporated into the tea itself (see page 15 on fruit teas) or used as a garnish by placing a slice in your cup. Its cleansing properties can repel negative energies while also improving your mood and giving you a boost if you have been feeling uninspired or unmotivated lately.

Orange (Sliced or as Juice)

Sweet and tangy oranges can help with cleansing, much like lemons. But this fruit has an even greater energetic punch, which can help promote creativity, inspire happiness, and make you feel strong and confident. Its revitalizing magical properties can bring you joy and help you conquer your fears.

Apple (Sliced or as Juice)

Apples have been cultivated for millennia, and there are more than 7,500 varieties. As fruit of the harvest, they have always symbolized abundance. If you don't have apple tea, putting a slice of apple (or a bit of apple juice) in your cup will add the apple's magical properties. Apples promote vitality, nurture the creative impulse, help love grow, and aid in the pursuit of knowledge.

Cinnamon

Cinnamon is used a lot in cooking, but it also happens to be a very powerful magical addition as well. It's used in many spells, and even just a sprinkle in your tea can give it a magical boost. A dash of cinnamon is good for healing, prosperity, success, happiness, and even love.

Nutmeg

Nutmeg has been used for centuries not only in cooking but also to attract money, health, luck, and good fortune. It was used by European witches in the past to heal their patients. It also enhances mental clarity and concentration, making it a good addition to your tea if you need to study. When using nutmeg, remember to never consume more than 1 teaspoon, since too much can be toxic. For your tea, I would only suggest using a small dash, as the taste is quite strong.

Allspice

Allspice is believed to ward off negativity and bad luck, making it a very useful spice for promoting happiness and good fortune. It's also known for its healing properties and was used as an antibacterial in folk medicine. It can even be used to enhance your connection to your intuition and boost your divination abilities.

Ginger

The energetic boost that ginger brings is powerful indeed. It carries with it the energy of fire and the sun, making it a revitalizing ingredient that will promote success, prosperity, and luck, and can help you let go of negative emotions like frustration, resentment, and jealousy.

Cloves

Cloves were regularly consumed in ancient Rome and China, where they were precious spices only the wealthy could afford. Because of that, cloves have always been associated with prosperity. Cloves have been used for banishing, purification, and protection spells for generations. They also stop gossip in its tracks and ward off negative energy. They can even help with love and good luck.

Star Anise

Star anise will help with mental clarity, dreams, and rest, which makes it a great spice to use for sleep or relaxation spells. It's also a great addition to courage and protection spells, as it is known to ward off negative energies. The scent of star anise is believed to help awaken psychic senses, so try some in your tea before a divination session.

Cardamom

Cardamom has been used for centuries as medicine, to season food, and even as a perfume. Its magical properties are tied to two planets, Mars and Venus. Its Mars energy means cardamom helps with concentration, confidence, courage, and health, and its Venus energy promotes passion, love, and self-love.

Mint

Mint has always been a magical plant. In Greek mythology, the water nymph Minthe was transformed into the mint plant by Persephone. The Romans used mint as a lucky charm. Adding a few mint leaves to your tea is not only delicious, but it will also promote abundance and prosperity, and help with decision-making and new beginnings. It's a great herb for motivation, protection, healing, and mindfulness.

creative combinations

With all these ingredients in mind, you can create interesting combinations of flavors and spells that include multiple simultaneous effects specific to your situation. For example, chamomile with a bit of honey will help with anxiety and stress even more than chamomile alone, as the added magical property of honey will give your cup an extra boost of happiness. Add in a bit of lemon and you will make your chamomile tea even more healing and calming: you'll find yourself relaxing and feeling comforted and warm, as if you are being protected by some outside force.

Have fun combining your base tea with sweeteners and other additions. A spell you enjoyed drinking is more likely to work, because your mindset heavily impacts your spellwork. If you had an awful time drinking your tea, it's harder to manifest your intentions. Because of that, taste is an essential part of a spell. Below are some ideas for mindfully mixing your ingredients.

Black Tea + Honey

Honey is a classic addition to a cup of tea. Paired with black tea, it will promote energy, happiness, and courage. Not a bad combination to sit down to every day.

Mint Tea + Brown Sugar

Combining mint tea and brown sugar is a great way to manifest comfort, sweetness, and healing. Use it at the end of a trying day.

Vanilla Tea + Cinnamon

Vanilla and cinnamon work well together in terms of both flavor profile and witchcraft. Together, their magical properties help with happiness, healing, and prosperity—perfect if you need a comforting drink after a hard day.

Matcha + Honey

A touch of honey can help sweeten matcha's bracing, vegetal taste while also promoting protection and healing. It's a great combination for happiness and courage, so if you need a bit of vigor before you start a tough project, this is a cup to consider.

Apple Tea + Cinnamon

Apple and cinnamon make for a comforting combo, perfect for cold weather. But it's also great for promoting abundance, creativity, and prosperity—truly the perfect tea to drink as the leaves start to fall.

Black Tea + Lemon

A slice of lemon in a cup of black tea is refreshing and will help with strength, energy, cleansing, and protection—a great way to start the day feeling energized and protected against negative energies.

Green Tea + Mint

When paired, these two flavors can help you manifest new beginnings and new energies and promote healing and mindfulness. When you're about to kick a bad habit or start a new routine, drink a glass of green tea with mint.

Vanilla Tea + Maple Syrup

Pouring a little bit of maple syrup in your vanilla tea will add a lovely touch of sweetness while promoting strength and prosperity. This is an encouraging and comforting drink, perfect for the cold weather.

Lavender Tea + Honey

By combining the cleansing powers of lavender with the healing properties of honey, you get a particularly soothing combo, great for helping with anxiety and stress and repelling negative energies.

Vanilla Tea + Honey

Both vanilla and honey promote happiness and strength, which makes them a highly compatible magical duo. Add to that the fact that honey's magic helps with courage and prosperity, while vanilla can bring you peace, and you get a very harmonious combo that can help with courage and happiness spells.

Orange Tea + Honey

Orange and honey form an amazing combo to boost your creativity. Orange helps with inspiration, success, and growth, while honey helps with passion and prosperity. It's an especially positive duo, as they both promote joy and happiness.

Lemon Tea + Honey

You've probably already mixed lemon with honey to help with a sore throat or the beginning of a cold. Lemon is purifying while honey is healing, so it's the perfect combo for taking care of both your body and your soul.

Black Tea + Maple Syrup

Black tea and maple syrup both promote strength and energy. The added advantage of this combo is that black tea is known for repelling negative energies, while maple syrup has protective proprieties, so it will also protect you from negativity.

Cinnamon Tea + Maple Syrup

This is another amazing combination for repelling negative energies, as cinnamon is known for banishing negativity, and both it and maple syrup are known for being protective and promoting success and good fortune.

Ginger Tea + Maple Syrup

Maple syrup symbolizes the resilience of nature and its ability to grow back after winter, and ginger's proprieties help you let go of anger and frustration. This is the perfect combination for you if you need some changes in your life or if you feel like it is time to let go of the things that no longer serve you.

Lemon Tea + Mint

Mint and lemon both possess cleansing and purifying powers. And with mint's magical properties helping with success and new beginnings, and lemon tea promoting protection, it's a great combination if you need extra help when facing a new chapter of your life.

Peach Tea + Mint

Peaches' magical properties promote harmony and can even ward off negative energies. Combined with the healing and protective powers of mint leaves, this combination is perfect for protection spells.

Ginger Tea + Mint

Much like with maple syrup, ginger tea combined with mint leaves will help you start fresh and approach things with a new outlook. Ginger promotes prosperity and helps you let go of negative emotions, and mint promotes new beginnings.

Orange Tea + Cinnamon

Orange tea and cinnamon both promote happiness and joy, making it a very good combination to help improve your mood. They also both represent success and prosperity, so it is a powerful duo if you need a boost in confidence or are trying to focus on your career or your studies. Add to that the creative properties of orange, and you get a great boost if you're feeling blocked creatively.

Black Tea + Ginger

This is one of the most energizing combos you can make, so it's perfect for your morning cup of tea. Revitalizing ginger gives you a magical boost and promotes prosperity. Combined with black tea's powers over strength and energy, and this duo will help you power through the day. They also both help repel negative thoughts and energies.

Cherry Tea + Brown Sugar

This is a powerful combination to promote love of all kinds. Brown sugar attracts both romantic love and friendship, and is a great way to sweeten your life. Cherries are known for their magical properties tied to love and passion. Combined, you have a potent duo. You can even use it to promote self-love, as brown sugar's healing properties will make cherry tea even more soft and soothing.

using moon water in your tea

What is moon water? Moon water is simply water that has been infused with the magical properties of the moon. Making it is quite easy, but the phases of the moon are very important and should always be taken into consideration. Each phase of the moon has a different magical property that can affect your spellwork accordingly.

Making moon water at home is simple.

1 Put tap or bottled water in a clean jar with a lid. Close the jar tightly.

2 Place the jar outside or on your windowsill under the light of the moon and leave it there for the whole night so it can charge.

3 Optional: you can charge the water itself before putting it under the moon by thinking or reciting out loud what your intent is with the water. Do you want abundance? Peace? Success? Put all of this in the water. It will make it more potent.

Moon water can be used in your bath water, to cleanse objects, or in spells, or it can be placed on an altar. It can also be used in tea magic! There are, of course, safety concerns when drinking water, especially if it was left outside for a few hours. This is why closing the jar is very important. You also cannot keep the moon water for longer than 1 week if you are planning on drinking it or using it on your skin, and always remember to boil it before consuming it.

To pick the moon phase mindfully and also achieve the best possible results when using the moon water in rituals and spellwork, use the moon correspondences below as a guide.

New Moon

The new moon is associated with new beginnings, fresh starts, and new cycles. This is a great moon water to use if you are looking for a new house or a new job, or if you're moving to a new country. This moon phase is the perfect blank canvas for your thoughts and your plans for the future.

Waxing Crescent Moon

The waxing moon is expanding, and so using waxing moon water will increase the effectiveness of your tea spells. This is also a great moon water to use for growth and self-development. Use it in luck, money, and career spells. This is the perfect moon phase for setting your intentions.

First Quarter Moon

The first quarter moon is all about taking action. If you are trying to attract and manifest things, use this water in your tea. First quarter moon water's magical properties help with creativity, motivation, and strength.

Waxing Gibbous Moon

The waxing gibbous moon is the perfect time to focus on your hopes and momentum. Using waxing gibbous moon water in your tea will attract success and courage, and it's a great water for an extra boost of motivation.

Full Moon

This is when the moon is at its peak and its magic is the most potent. If you're looking to give your spell a little energy boost, this is the water to use. The full moon is the time to harvest the intentions you have set during previous phases. Use this moon water for strength, love, protection, and health.

Waning Gibbous Moon

The waning gibbous moon is a time for introspection, so use this water in cleansing spells and banishing spells. It is also a good moon phase for closure and turning pages on chapters of your life that need to stay in the past.

Third Quarter Moon

The third quarter moon is the time to release and let go of things that no longer serve you. It's a great moon water to use if you're looking to break bad habits, and its magical properties are calming and cleansing.

Waning Crescent Moon

The waning crescent moon is all about decreasing. When you want things to leave you, vanish, or go away, use moon water from this phase. It's perfect for cleansing yourself of bad energies, stress, habits that don't serve you, and beliefs that limit you. This moon phase is also the time to rest, and it can be good for sleeping and relaxing spells.

Each phase of the moon influences the water, and so it's important to pick your moon water accordingly.

However, you can use always full moon water as a replacement when needed, as it is the most potent moon water and will always boost your spellwork.

tea-making rituals

Even the ritual of making tea can add to your spell. For example, you can stir your tea clockwise to attract good fortune. Try to think about what you would like to attract that day as you stir. Happiness? Success? A stress-free day? Adding a clear intent will boost your manifestation. Alternately, you can also stir your tea counterclockwise to banish bad things from your day, like negativity and anxiety.

If you are familiar with sigils, you can draw one in your tea with your spoon. A sigil is a symbol created to invoke an intention, like self-love, protection, or power. You can create your own or find already existing sigils online. If you like your tea in the morning, I suggest using sigils for energy or motivation. And if you prefer drinking herbal tea at night, you might try using sigils for peace, protection, or sleep.

Adding mindful elements to your cup is the first step toward spellwork. In fact, a cup of tea with a splash of milk and a bit of honey can be a small, simple spell on its own, as long as the intent is there. Consideration for every ingredient, as well as your method of brewing, will add strength to your original intent and subtly affect its capabilities.

HONEY
for happiness

MINT
for abundance

ORANGE TEA
for joy

LEMON
for energy

4

spells to
COZY UP TO

NOW THAT WE have explored the basics and magical properties of tea and other ingredients, it is time to properly dive into tea witchcraft.

And what better way to do it than with spells? In this chapter, you will find more than twenty tea spells that you can try at home. They have a variety of different effects, like relaxation, courage, and self-love. Of course, this doesn't represent the full range of spells that you can do with tea, but should give you a good basis for understanding the different ways it can be used. There's also a section at the end of this chapter detailing how you can create your own tea spell.

This chapter will also include original ways to use tea leaves in your spell-work, no matter which type of witchcraft you practice.

a few tea spells

A quick note before we dive into this collection of spells: when following a spell, you can always swap out ingredients according to your taste or dietary restrictions, or even according to what you have in your pantry. Just remember to be mindful of the magical properties of the ingredient you are using, as it still needs to work with your intent. If you're not sure about a swap, check the tea correspondences section starting on page 11.

When it comes to brewing tea, each tea is different, and some of us like our cup stronger than others. Don't worry, though—the brewing time will not affect your spells, so feel free steep your tea for as long as you prefer or according to each tea's instructions.

Remember to always boil moon water it before drinking it, and store it in a tightly sealed jar in the fridge for no longer than 1 week.

— CHAMOMILE TEA SPELL —
FOR A GOOD NIGHT'S SLEEP

INGREDIENTS

....

CHAMOMILE TEA, *for sleep and relaxation*

SOY MILK, *for protection*

HONEY, *for happiness and to relieve stress*

NUTMEG, *for comfort*

CINNAMON, *for healing*

1. Steep the chamomile tea in hot water for a few minutes, then remove the tea leaves.

2. Add a splash of soy milk.

3. Add a spoon of honey, a sprinkle of nutmeg, and a sprinkle of cinnamon, to taste.

4. Stir the tea counterclockwise to repel bad dreams and anxiety.

This very simple tea spell is great if you have trouble sleeping or have been struggling with anxiety. We all know that when life gets a little bit too stressful, it can impact our sleep drastically, keeping us awake at night, tossing and turning until morning while rehashing the same negative thoughts. If you need a good's night sleep to recharge, this spell is for you. Chamomile, known for its relaxing properties, and honey, an ingredient packed with happiness and positivity, is the perfect combo to help you sleep, and milk will add a little touch of comfort. You can swap out the soy milk for cow's milk, which is also a very protective and nurturing milk. If you need another plant-based option, you can use other milks, but be mindful of their magical properties. For this spell, coconut milk or hazelnut milk are also great substitutions.

This recipe calls for only a little sprinkle of nutmeg, as the taste can be quite overpowering—remember, never consume more than 1 teaspoon of nutmeg.

— BLACK TEA SPELL —
FOR COURAGE

INGREDIENTS
....

BLACK TEA, *for strength, any variety: Ceylon, Darjeeling, or even a breakfast blend*

GINGER SLICES OR POWDERED GINGER, *optional, for an energy boost*

ALMOND MILK, *to tackle new goals*

CINNAMON, *for power*

1. Steep the black tea and one ginger slice, if using, in hot water for a few minutes. (You can add two slices of ginger if you like a stronger taste, though I would not advise adding more than two slices—you lose the taste of the tea!) Remove the tea leaves and ginger slices, if using.

2. Add a splash of almond milk.

3. Add a sprinkle of cinnamon, to taste.

4. If you did not brew the tea with ginger slices, add a sprinkle of ginger powder, to taste, if desired.

5. Stir the tea clockwise to attract power and courage.

Prepare this tea spell whenever you need an extra boost of courage. This brew is perfect for the first day of school, when you're starting a new job, or if you're trying something that might be a little bit nerve-racking. Black tea is known for being the strongest of teas, not only because of its taste but also because of its magical properties. It's the ideal tea when you need extra courage. Almond milk is potent and great for abundance, luck, and helping you achieve new goals. Goat milk is another good option, as it's known to help with power and success—that way, you'll get over the jitters you're feeling and be on your way to achieving great things.

— VANILLA TEA SPELL —
FOR JOY

INGREDIENTS
....

**VANILLA
BLACK TEA**, *for
happiness and
self-love*

ALMOND MILK,
for abundance

HONEY, *for joy*

CINNAMON,
*to boost your
happiness*

A JOY SIGIL.
*You can use
this one, or find
another one
that works best
for you.*

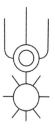

1. Steep the vanilla black tea in hot water for a few minutes, then remove the tea leaves.

2. Add a splash of almond milk.

3. Add a spoonful of honey.

4. Add a sprinkle of cinnamon, to taste.

5. Stir clockwise to attract joy and happiness.

6. With the spoon, draw the joy sigil in the tea.

If you need an extra dose of joy, this is the perfect tea spell for you. Or maybe you've been feeling a little bit down, and need a little bit of joy infused in your daily life. Either way, this tea spell is ideal for starting the day on the right foot. Black tea will keep you energized while banishing bad energies, and honey and cinnamon symbolize happiness, joy, and abundance. You can swap honey for brown sugar if you prefer, as the sugar will add an extra note of comfort and sweetness. Most milks work well with abundance, so choose the one that is to your liking.

Drawing a sigil with a spoon may seem daunting, but it's really all about the intention. It's less about creating the perfect representation of the symbol and more about focusing your thoughts on its appearance as you move the spoon. This is also an opportunity to use a different sigil if you'd like to

alter the intent of the spell, or even create your own. If you want to use another sigil, you can find plenty online. Just remember to credit a sigil's creator if one is listed, especially if you are going to share the spell on social media. This particular sigil was created by me and is my offering to you. I hope it helps you see the blessings already around you, particularly on days when that seems difficult.

— MANGO AND LEMON TEA SPELL —
FOR GOOD LUCK

INGREDIENTS
....

WAXING CRESCENT MOON WATER, *for luck, or regular water*

MANGO TEA, *for luck*

HONEY, *for happiness*

A SLICE OF LEMON, *for protection*

1. Boil the moon water. Pour the boiled water into a teacup.

2. Steep the mango tea in the moon water for a few minutes, then remove the tea leaves.

3. Add a spoonful of honey.

4. Add a slice of lemon.

We all need a little bit of luck sometimes. Maybe life has seemed to have an endless supply of bad news lately, or perhaps you just want an extra touch of luck for an exam, a promotion, or another important event. Whatever the reason is, this tea spell will attract good fortune your way. Mangos are a symbol of joy and luck, and lemon, perfect for protection, will keep any bad luck at bay. This tea is delicious hot or cold. If you want to drink it cold, follow the same steps but finish by putting it into a shaker with some ice. If you don't have mango tea, you can use strawberry or pineapple tea, which are also great for luck. If you don't have any fruit tea at home, you can add some mango slices or syrup to your tea, but remember to be mindful of the magical properties of the base tea you pick. This spell is perfect for an extra boost of good luck.

— GINSENG TEA SPELL —

FOR ATTRACTING MONEY YOUR WAY

INGREDIENTS
....

WAXING CRESCENT MOON WATER, *to attract money,* or *regular water*

GINSENG TEA, *for success*

A SLICE OF APPLE, *for prosperity*

MAPLE SYRUP, *for prosperity*

1. Boil the moon water. Pour the boiled water into a teacup.

2. Brew the ginseng tea with the apple slice in the moon water for a few minutes, then remove the tea leaves. You can remove the apple slice or leave it in the cup.

3. Add maple syrup, to taste.

4. Stir clockwise to attract money and success.

If you want to attract money your way, this is the spell for you. In general, money spells work best if you know how you want to manifest your money. Do you have a small business? Are you a freelancer? Are you applying for a new job? Keep your specific goal in mind when drinking this tea.

Apples are symbols of the abundance of the harvest and are associated with success and prosperity, which makes them the perfect fruit for this spell. If you don't have apples, you can use apple juice instead; it won't affect the magical effect. Ginseng tea is known for promoting passion, success, and energy. But if you don't have ginseng tea, you can substitute ginger or cinnamon tea, which both have similar qualities that align them with prosperity and success.

— LAVENDER TEA SPELL —
AGAINST ANXIETY

INGREDIENTS
....

COW'S MILK OR RICE MILK, *for protection*

LAVENDER TEA, *to repel negativity*

VANILLA EXTRACT, *for self-love*

HONEY, *for protection and healing*

1. On the stovetop over low heat, gently warm the milk and lavender tea. Don't let the milk boil! Once the lavender tea has steeped to your liking, remove the tea leaves.

2. Add a few drops of vanilla extract and stir.

3. Pour the lavender milk tea into a cup.

4. Add a spoonful of honey.

5. Stir the milk tea counterclockwise to repel anxiety and negativity.

When struggling with anxiety, it can be hard to function throughout the day, and falling asleep at night can be difficult, too. It's so easy to get caught up on negative thoughts, which can make us feel powerless or even frozen. This simple and comforting tea spell should help you when you need an extra boost of strength to fight anxious thoughts. You can use it to help you during an overall stressful period, or you can even use it to fight panic attacks if you are prone to them. Lavender is known for its deeply relaxing properties, and when paired with honey (nature's most magical happiness booster) in this spell, it is sure to wrap you in a comforting blanket. If you're not a fan of honey, you can use brown sugar instead, as it also promotes healing

and comfort. Vanilla extract is usually the more convenient option as we often already have it in our pantry, but if you have vanilla beans, feel free to use those in the spell instead. Simply infuse the milk with them while the tea is brewing.

FOR GIVING YOUR MAGIC A BOOST

INGREDIENTS
....

FULL MOON WATER, *the most potent moon water*

DANDELION TEA, *for a magic boost*

MINT LEAVES, *for abundance*

A SLICE OF LEMON, *ruled by the moon*

1. Boil the moon water. For this spell, using full moon water is important. Pour the boiled water into a teacup.

2. Steep the dandelion tea in the boiled moon water, then remove the tea leaves.

3. Add a few mint leaves and crush them slightly with your spoon.

4. Squeeze the slice of lemon into the tea, then add the slice.

5. Stir the tea clockwise to attract what you want to manifest with your spell.

This tea spell is perfect for boosting your magic or another spell that needs some extra energy. The full moon is known for being the most potent phase of the moon and is usually the perfect time to do spellwork. But because we can't always do our spells during a full moon, this tea is here to bring you the full moon's magic properties whenever you need them. As always, remember to boil your moon water first, and never keep it in the fridge for longer than 1 week. All the ingredients of this spell are tied to the moon, but don't worry—if you don't have dandelion tea, you can use lemon or watermelon tea, as both those fruits are also ruled by the moon. You

can drink this tea before doing some spellwork or whenever you feel like your magic needs a little bit of help. It's also the perfect tea spell to sip while working on your book of shadows, if you have one.

— APPLE AND ORANGE TEA SPELL —
FOR CREATIVITY

INGREDIENTS
....

FIRST QUARTER MOON WATER, *for your imagination, or regular water*

APPLE TEA, *for creativity and abundance*

CINNAMON, *for creativity*

THE ZEST OF HALF AN ORANGE, *for creativity*

1. Boil the moon water on the stovetop.

2. Add the apple tea, a sprinkle of cinnamon, and the orange zest to the pan.

3. Stir clockwise to attract creativity and imagination.

4. Once steeped to your liking, strain the tea into a cup and enjoy.

Having artist's block? Writer's block? *Any* creativity blocks? This tea spell is for you! We all know the stress of the white page. As an artist myself, I know that there is nothing more frustrating than wanting to create but being hit by a wall of blockages. Now, we all have our own techniques to fight the creative block. Whether you like to power through it or recharge, this spell will help boost your inspiration and your creativity. Apples, cinnamon, and oranges are known for boosting creativity, which makes them the perfect combo for this spell. First quarter moon water is a great addition, as it boosts your inspiration, but you can use regular water if you don't have any on hand.

— SUN TEA SPELL —
FOR ENERGY

ORANGE TEA, *for joy and confidence*

HONEY, *for happiness*

A WHOLE LEMON, SLICED, *for energy*

A FEW MINT LEAVES, *for abundance*

1. Add cold water to a clean glass pitcher or bottle. Don't fill it to the top—you'll need room for the ingredients.

2. Add the orange tea. Depending on the size of your pitcher, you might need two or three tea bags.

3. Add the lemon slices and mint leaves. Stir the mixture.

4. Leave the pitcher or bottle under direct sunlight for 2 hours. Keep it tightly shut, especially if you are leaving it outside. If you prefer to avoid sun brewing your tea, place the pitcher directly in the refrigerator; the tea will infuse in a couple of hours.

5. Refrigerate for about 1 hour to finish steeping, then remove the tea bags.

6. Add a spoonful of honey and stir.

7. Use the tea within 8 hours of refrigeration.

With this tea spell, you are using the warmth and energy of the sun to brew your tea. This technique allows the sun to imbue your tea with its magical properties: success, ambition, joy, confidence, and vitality. This spell is particularly helpful if you have been struggling feeling motivated, need a boost of energy, or have been feeling low on morale. I mean,

what better than the power of the sun to recharge your happiness? Just like there is something magical about lying under the sun to let its warmth energize and comfort us, there is something magical about this sun tea. This tea is best enjoyed cold—it's perfect for the summer. Store it in the refrigerator for up to 8 hours; after that, throw away any unused tea to prevent the growth of bacteria in the water.

— HEALING TEA SPELL —
FOR THE SOUL

INGREDIENTS
....

CINNAMON BLACK TEA, for *protection*

OAT MILK, for *healing*

HONEY, for *happiness*

A SLICE OF APPLE, for *abundance and health*

1. Steep the cinnamon tea in hot water for a few minutes, then remove the tea leaves.

2. Add a splash of oat milk.

3. Add a spoonful of honey and the apple slice.

4. Stir clockwise to attract comfort and peace, or counterclockwise to repel negativity.

This healing tea spell is meant to soothe your soul and appease your worries. Some days, we just need that extra bit of healing. While we often take time to take care of our body, our mind needs just as much attention. It's easy to keep going until we burn ourselves out. So, take some time during your day to take care of your soul, too, with this soothing tea spell. The sweetness of honey and the comforting taste of cinnamon work in tandem, helping you to forget your anxiety, if only temporarily. If you don't have oat milk, which helps with healing, you can use cow's milk or soy milk instead; both are known for their soothing and comforting properties. If you don't have apples, which promote vitality, you can use apple juice instead; it won't affect the spell.

— MATCHA LATTE TEA SPELL —
FOR PROTECTION

INGREDIENTS:
....

MATCHA POWDER, *for healing and protection*

COW'S MILK OR SOY MILK, *for protection*

HONEY, *for protection and courage*

A PROTECTION SIGIL. *You can use this one, or find another one that works best for you!*

1. Whisk the matcha powder with a little bit of hot water.

2. Warm the milk, then add it to the matcha.

3. Add honey, to taste, and stir.

4. With the spoon, draw the sigil in the tea.

This matcha latte is the perfect protection spell if you're craving something warm and comforting. Let it wrap you in its warm, reassuring feeling like a cozy blanket, while it keeps negativity at bay. Whether you are trying to face a fear or you have been feeling nervous and anxious because of life events, this spell will bring you a much-needed moment of comfort and protection. While a bamboo whisk or a frother is more traditional for combining the matcha with the water, if you don't have one, you can use a regular whisk.

You can swap honey for brown sugar, which is good for healing.

Drawing a sigil with a spoon can look daunting, but it's really all about the intention. If you want another sigil, you can find plenty online. Just remember to credit the creator of the sigil if one is listed. This particular sigil was created by me and is a protective offering meant to ward off bad energies.

This latte is delicious hot, but if you prefer, it's easily turned into an iced matcha latte. Simply use cold milk and add some ice cubes.

SPELLS TO COZY UP TO

— MEDITATION TEA SPELL —

FOR CLAIRVOYANCE AND PEACE

INGREDIENTS
....

WANING CRESCENT MOON WATER, *for relaxation and cleansing, or regular water*

SAGE TEA, *for grounding*

A SLICE OF LEMON, *for cleansing*

A FEW MINT LEAVES, *for mindfulness*

1. Boil the moon water. Pour the boiled water into a teacup.

2. Brew the sage tea to your liking, then remove the tea leaves.

3. Squeeze the lemon slice then add it to the cup. Stir clockwise.

4. Add the mint leaves.

5. Stir clockwise again to attract peace. Stir counterclockwise to repel negativity.

Meditating is a great grounding exercise, and grounding is an important part of witchcraft: it allows you to be more in tune with yourself and the universe around you. Whether you are using meditation as a tool to fight anxiety, to feel more centered inside your body, or to prepare before divination, this is the perfect spell for you. With this simple tea spell, you can enhance your meditative experience. Sage tea's grounding and cleansing properties will help you center yourself before meditating. Waning crescent moon water will help you cleanse yourself of bad energies and stress. As always, when using moon water, remember to boil it and to never keep it longer than 1 week in your fridge. If you don't have sage tea, you can use oolong tea, which in

witchcraft has often been connected to meditation and divination, as it promotes both wisdom and concentration.

— SUMMER TEA SPELL —
FOR VITALITY AND STRENGTH

INGREDIENTS
....

BLACK TEA, *for strength and energy*

HONEY, *for happiness*

A SLICE OF LEMON, *for energy*

STRAWBERRY SLICES OR SYRUP, *for strength and joy*

1. Add cold water to a clean glass pitcher or bottle. Don't fill it to the top; you'll need room for the ingredients.

2. Add the black tea. Depending on the size of your pitcher, you might need two or three tea bags.

3. Add the lemon slice and strawberry slices or syrup. Stir to combine.

4. Leave the pitcher or bottle under direct sunlight for 2 hours. Keep it tightly shut, especially if you are leaving it outside! If you prefer to avoid sun brewing your tea, place the pitcher directly in the refrigerator; the tea will infuse in a couple of hours.

5. Refrigerate for 1 hour to finish steeping, then remove the tea bags.

6. Add a spoonful of honey and stir.

7. Use sun-brewed tea within 8 hours of refrigeration.

This iced tea spell is perfect for the summer. In pagan witchcraft, the summer solstice (called Litha) is a celebration of the sun and its powers. Litha marks the longest day and the shortest night of the year. We get the most sunlight, and it's a celebration of summer, sunshine, and warmth. Nature is ripe with abundance and prosperity. You can celebrate Litha by baking cakes with honey (a symbol

of the summer equinox), watching the sunset, making a sunflower wreath, harvesting and drying herbs, or having a picnic with your loved ones. But even if you don't celebrate Litha, this tea spell will help boost your summer with vitality and strength. Brewing tea with the sun is a great way to infuse more magic into it, but feel free to infuse it normally if you prefer. If you have used the sun brewing technique, store it in the refrigerator for up to 8 hours; after that, throw away any unused tea to prevent the growth of bacteria in the water.

— FALL TEA SPELL —
FOR ABUNDANCE

INGREDIENTS
....

EARL GREY TEA, *for abundance*

COW'S MILK OR ALMOND MILK, *for prosperity*

CINNAMON, *for protection and prosperity*

GROUND GINGER, *for prosperity and success*

NUTMEG, *for luck and good fortune*

ALLSPICE, *for luck and abundance*

MAPLE SYRUP, *for prosperity*

1. Brew the Earl Grey tea in hot water for a few minutes, then remove the tea leaves.

2. Add a splash of milk.

3. Add a sprinkle of cinnamon, a sprinkle of ground ginger, a sprinkle of nutmeg, and a sprinkle of allspice, to taste.

4. Add a little bit of maple syrup, to taste.

5. Stir clockwise to attract the abundance of the harvest.

Fall is the time to harvest. It's the season of abundance and prosperity and the perfect moment to reap the rewards of your hard work. In pagan witchcraft, the autumn equinox (called Mabon) is the harvest festival. Traditionally, people knew at the fall equinox if the harvest had been good and would sustain them through winter. In fall, the days are getting shorter and colder. Nature is getting ready for winter, and so should you. It's an opportunity to try to let go of the things that don't serve you anymore, while being grateful for what you do have. To celebrate Mabon you can go apple picking, visit a pumpkin patch, take a stroll through the woods, or bake fall treats like pumpkin or apple pies. But even if you don't celebrate Mabon, attract

abundance your way with this tea spell, which also happens to be the perfect fall drink! If you don't have maple syrup, you can substitute brown sugar for a little touch of comfort.

This recipe calls for only a little sprinkle of nutmeg, as the taste can be quite overpowering—remember, never consume more than 1 teaspoon of nutmeg.

— WINTER TEA SPELL —
FOR CLEANSING AND INTROSPECTION

INGREDIENTS

....

CINNAMON TEA, *for healing and to banish negative energy*

ORANGE SLICES, *for purification and cleansing*

GINGER SLICES OR GROUND GINGER, *to let go of frustration*

VANILLA EXTRACT, *for self-love*

1. On the stovetop, boil some water in a pan.

2. Steep the cinnamon tea in the pan with a couple of orange slices and the ginger.

3. Add a few drops of vanilla extract. Stir counterclockwise to banish negative energy.

4. Strain the tea into a cup and enjoy.

Winter is a time for rest, reflection, and introspection. In pagan witchcraft, the winter solstice (called Yule) represents rebirth and new beginnings. Nature is asleep, and you can cleanse yourself of the stress accumulated during the year. It's the longest night of the year, symbolizing the return of light after a long winter. You can celebrate Yule by baking and decorating a yule log cake (symbolizing the log that kept your home warm throughout the longest night), making a wreath, handmaking some gifts for your family and friends, or volunteering for a charity of your choice. Even if you don't celebrate Yule, drink this this warm and comforting tea spell to repel all the negative energy and turn to a new page in preparation for spring. If you don't have cinnamon tea you can use another tea (I would suggest a white tea or a peppermint tea), but if you do that, add a sprinkle of cinnamon to the recipe when you add the oranges and ginger.

— SPRING TEA SPELL —
FOR FERTILITY AND RENEWAL

INGREDIENTS
....

WAXING CRESCENT MOON WATER, *for growth, or regular water*

LEMON BALM TEA, *for happiness and healing*

A LEMON SLICE, *for protection and cleansing*

MINT LEAVES, *for new energies and new beginnings*

1. Boil the moon water. Pour the boiled water into a teacup.

2. Steep the lemon balm tea to your liking, then remove the tea leaves.

3. Squeeze the lemon slice, then add it to the cup. Stir clockwise.

4. Add mint leaves.

5. Stir clockwise again, to attract new energies.

Spring is a time for renewal and rebirth. In pagan witchcraft, the spring equinox (called Ostara) celebrates the fertility of spring. Spring returns after the winter, bringing in its path a bustling nature filled with plants, fruits, vegetables, and wildlife awakening from hibernation. You can celebrate Ostara by decorating eggs (a symbol of fertility and the return of spring), doing your spring cleaning, gardening, or filling your home with bouquets of flowers. But even if you don't celebrate Ostara, you can drink this tea spell to open yourself to new possibilities and new beginnings. Waxing crescent moon water is perfect for setting new intentions and helping with self-development. As always when using moon water, remember to boil it and to never keep it longer than 1 week in your fridge. If you don't have lemon balm tea, you can use lemon tea instead.

— ROOIBOS TEA SPELL —

FOR BOOSTING YOUR CONFIDENCE

INGREDIENTS
....

ROOIBOS TEA,
for confidence

ALMOND MILK,
to achieve your goals

NUTMEG, *for confidence*

CINNAMON, *for success*

MAPLE SYRUP, *for strength*

1. Steep the rooibos tea to your liking, then remove the tea leaves.

2. Add a splash of almond milk.

3. Add a sprinkle of nutmeg and a sprinkle of cinnamon, to taste.

4. Add a little bit of maple syrup, to taste.

With its ability to grant determination, strength, and courage, rooibos is the perfect tea to boost your confidence! This rooibos latte spell will give you all the confidence and drive to achieve your goals and believe in yourself. And because rooibos has no caffeine, you can make this spell any time of day. You never know when you might need to feel bold and intrepid. Whether you are nervous about a work presentation in the morning or going onstage at night to perform in a play, a cup of this rooibos latte will give you the assurance you need. If you don't have or don't like almond milk, you can use cow's milk instead, which will promote abundance and prosperity.

This recipe calls for only a little sprinkle of nutmeg, as the taste can be quite overpowering—remember, never consume more than 1 teaspoon of nutmeg.

— HOT CHOCOLATE SPELL —
FOR SELF-LOVE

INGREDIENTS
....

**COW'S MILK OR
ALMOND MILK,**
for abundance

**POWDERED
CHOCOLATE,**
*for self-love
(can be dark or
milk chocolate)*

CINNAMON,
*for happiness
and love*

**VANILLA
EXTRACT,** *for
self-love*

1. In a pan on the stovetop, gently heat the milk. Do not allow it to boil.

2. Add 2 heaping teaspoons of powdered chocolate and stir clockwise.

3. Add a sprinkle of cinnamon.

4. Add a few drops of vanilla extract.

5. Stir clockwise to attract self-love, and counterclockwise to banish negative thoughts about yourself.

6. Pour the hot chocolate in a cup and enjoy!

This warm and comforting spell is all about self-love. Hot chocolate is the perfect hot beverage for love: it's rich and sweet, and with its decadent and luxurious taste inviting indulgence, chocolate's magical properties help promote self-love. Hot chocolate, much like a box of chocolate, is a lovely treat. And just like you would give chocolate to a loved one, give yourself a nice little present with this spell. If you'd prefer to use chocolate and not powdered chocolate for this recipe, go for it! It should give the hot chocolate a richer, more decadent taste. Simply melt a few pieces of chocolate in the milk.

Vanilla extract, a spice tied to love and happiness, will give the spell an extra boost. It's usually the

more convenient option because we often already
have it in the pantry, but if you have vanilla beans,
feel free to use those in the spell instead. Simply
infuse the milk with it like you would normally.

SPELLS TO COZY UP TO

— COFFEE AND MINT LATTE SPELL —
FOR MOTIVATION

INGREDIENTS
....

COFFEE, *for motivation and energy (you can use instant coffee or any coffee you usually drink)*

HONEY, *for courage*

MINT SYRUP, *for motivation*

OAT MILK, *for prosperity*

1. Prepare the coffee the way you usually do.

2. Add a spoonful of honey and dash of mint syrup. Stir clockwise.

3. Add a splash of oat milk. You can warm it up first, if you like.

4. Stir clockwise to attract energy and motivation.

Mint and coffee can seem like a surprising combo, but it's actually really good. Coffee is a powerful way to awaken you and your motivation, and it is known in witchcraft for sparking inspiration. Mint helps with decision-making and abundance. It's the perfect magical duo for motivation! If you're really not a fan of mint but need some oomph to help you reach your goals, you can use vanilla syrup (which will boost your happiness) or cinnamon syrup (which will usher in success) instead.

This can be made hot or cold . . . both are delicious, and also will put a bit of pep in your step. For an iced coffee, simply pour the ingredients into a shaker with ice, shake, and then pour it back into a glass or a cup.

— OOLONG TEA SPELL —
FOR DIVINATION

INGREDIENTS
....

OOLONG TEA,
*for divination
and focus*

NUTMEG, *for
clarity*

APPLE SLICES,
for knowledge

HONEY, *for
healing*

SOY MILK, *for
spirituality*

1. On the stovetop, boil some water.

2. Add the tea, a pinch of nutmeg (not a lot—the taste is very strong), and a couple of apple slices. Stir.

3. Let the tea and other ingredients infuse to your liking before removing the pan from the heat.

4. Strain the tea into a cup. You can add the apple slices to the cup or leave them out.

5. Add honey, to taste, and stir.

6. Add the soy milk (can be added warm or cold), and stir clockwise to attract focus.

This tea will help you focus and ground yourself, and it is the perfect spell if you're looking to boost your divination abilities. I believe that divination is above all the art of reaching into our subconscious and listening to our intuition to feel and understand what the future might hold. Oolong is known for promoting wisdom and helping you connect with your intuition, making it the perfect tea for this spell. However, if you don't have any oolong tea, you can use a pu-erh tea instead, which is known for helping develop divination abilities, or even a dandelion tea, a healing and grounding option. While soy milk is perfect for helping you get in touch with your subconscious, hazelnut milk is a good option if

you don't like soy milk. However, hazelnut milk is a lot sweeter, so you might need to adjust the quantity of honey you use.

This recipe calls for only a pinch of nutmeg, as the taste can be quite overpowering—remember, never consume more than 1 teaspoon of nutmeg.

If you're trying tea leaf reading (see chapter 5 to learn more about tasseomancy), using oolong tea is a great option!

SPELLS TO COZY UP TO

make your own tea spell

Maybe you need a spell for a specific intent you haven't found in this book, or maybe you just want to try coming up with your own tea spell recipe. By now, you should have a pretty good idea of how to approach a basic spell using tea, so you have the tools to structure your own for your own specific situation. Here are a few pointers:

- ❧ **PICK THE INGREDIENTS MINDFULLY.** Each ingredient needs to serve a purpose and be in alignment with your intent (find ingredient correspondences in chapters 2 and 3). For instance, avoid picking a tea known for promoting energy if you're trying to create a sleeping spell.

- ❧ **DON'T FORGET ABOUT THE TASTE!** Yes, the ingredients all need to work together to help you manifest what you want, but they also need to taste good together. With tea witchcraft, taste is just as important as intent. Drinking your spell should be a warm, comforting experience.

- ❧ **TRY, TRY, AND TRY AGAIN.** Not all spells are going to work like you want them to right away. Some spells might work for others but not work for you. If you try a spell and it doesn't give you the result you hoped for, make some changes and try again. I advise keeping a notebook where you can write down your own spells, their effects, and any changes you might make. This advice applies anytime you're trying other people's spells (like the spells in this book). If something doesn't work for you, adjust and keep track of your changes.

Now that you know all that, what are the different elements of a tea spell? While you can always experiment with spellmaking, there are a few key ingredients that a tea spell should have.

1 TEA: Obviously, this will be the core of your spell. Using the tea correspondences in chapter 2, pick the right tea for your spell: black tea for energy, white tea for wisdom, etc.

2 MILK: Milk is optional, but it can add a magical boost to your spell. Milk won't taste good with every tea, so remember to think about your spell's overall taste. Using the milk correspondences in chapter 3, you can pick the perfect milk for your intent.

3 MAGICAL ADDITIONS: Magical additions can be spices, fruits, honey . . . anything you add to your tea will be an important part of your tea spell. You can go with a classic ingredient like honey if you need help with happiness, or you can add a pinch of nutmeg for confidence. You can use the correspondence chart in chapter 3 to help you pick your magical additions!

4 **MOON WATER**: Like milk, moon water is optional. Steeping tea in hot moon water will infuse your tea with the magical energy of the moon. Pick the moon phase carefully using the moon correspondences in chapter 3.

5 **SIGILS**: Sigils are also optional, but they can seal in your intent. You can find an existing sigil online or make your own. Once you have chosen your sigil, you can either "draw" it in your tea with your spoon or physically mark it on your cup if you'd like it to be there every time you have a drink.

6 **PREPARATION**: The preparation of a spell is also important. Are you brewing the tea on the stove or in a cup? Are you stirring clockwise or counterclockwise? All these elements will help you perfect your spell when it comes to taste and its magical efficacy.

Remember to have fun with this process, and do not get discouraged if your spells don't work right away. Just keep trying. Regardless of whether you achieve the desired effect with your spell, you'll at least be able to enjoy delicious tea!

other ways to use tea
in your spellwork

The most obvious way to use tea or tea leaves in your spellwork, of course, is to brew and drink the tea. But there are other ways to incorporate this powerful ingredient into your workings, whether you are a kitchen witch, a bath witch, an eclectic witch, or a beginner.

My favorite way to use tea differently is with bath witchcraft. Bath witchcraft consists of infusing bath water with herbs and oils, lighting candles, and perhaps playing some nature sounds or music to turn your bath into its own spell. It transforms a simple mundane gesture like taking a bath into a true ritual dedicated to you and your magic. It's a chance to relax, take care of yourself, and do some spellwork.

To use tea in your bath, simply put some tea bags into your bath water and let it infuse. If you like using loose tea leaves, place them in a tea ball, a muslin or organza bag, or an empty tea bag to avoid a mess. I would suggest using two or three tea bags. You can use the tea correspondences listed in chapter 2 to pick the right blend for your intent. For example, chamomile tea will make your bath extra relaxing, which is perfect after a long day, while lemon tea will add cleansing properties to the water.

I hope these different examples will inspire you to incorporate tea in your spellwork. It is a versatile ingredient with so many different magical properties, and the vast variety of different teas and herbal tisanes means that you're likely to find one for any goal you are trying to manifest. And of course, don't hesitate to get creative and come up with your own spells with tea leaves.

— RELAXING CHAMOMILE BATH SPELL —
FOR A MOMENT OF PEACE

INGREDIENTS
....

2 OR 3 CHAMOMILE TEA BAGS, *for calmness*

A FEW TABLESPOONS OF DRIED LAVENDER, *for relaxation*

A TEA BALL, SMALL ORGANZA OR MUSLIN DRAWSTRING POUCH, OR EMPTY TEA BAG, *to contain the lavender*

A COUPLE OF CANDLES; *white, blue, and purple are colors that are aligned with relaxation*

ANYTHING YOU MIGHT FIND RELAXING DURING YOUR BATH, *such as a book, a wireless speaker playing soothing music, a bath pillow, a cup of tea (such as chamomile or lavender), and so on*

1. Start by drawing a warm bath.

2. Put the chamomile tea bags in the water.

3. Add the bag with the dried lavender.

4. Light the candles, being careful to place them in a safe place where you won't burn yourself.

5. Take your bath and enjoy!

If you don't have a bathtub, don't worry! You can tie the teabags to your shower-head, infusing the water with the proper-ties of the tea as it flows onto your skin. Whether you're using tea bags in your bath or in the shower, be sure to throw them out afterward. After being used in this way, they won't be suitable for an additional steep and their magical proper-ties are also spent.

— WHITE TEA PROTECTION JAR —
FOR WARDING OFF NEGATIVE ENERGY

INGREDIENTS

A CLEAN JAR WITH A LID

A FUNNEL

CHILI FLAKES, *to banish undesired energies*

WHITE TEA LEAVES, *either loose or removed from a tea bag, for protection*

SALT, *for cleansing and to absorb negative energies*

BLACK PEPPER, *to banish negative energies*

A PROTECTION SIGIL

A SMALL PIECE OF PAPER

A PEN, PREFERABLY BLACK

A WHITE OR BLACK CANDLE, *to seal the jar*

1. Start by cleansing the jar and the funnel. Cleansing in this case means ridding the object of any lingering energies so that it can be a blank canvas for your spell. There are different ways to cleanse in witchcraft. For example, you can use water (but make sure to dry everything thoroughly before using) or you can use incense smoke.

2. Using the funnel, put the ingredients in the jar in order: start with the chili flakes, then the tea, the salt, and finally the pepper. For each ingredient, think about its magical properties and how they will help protect you. For instance, you can ask the chili flakes to banish undesired energies from your home. You can call upon individual ingredients that way, each time asking them to apply their magical properties.

3. Draw the sigil on the piece of paper. I would suggest using a black pen for protection, but any pen will work.

4. Fold the piece of paper and put it in the jar, then screw on the lid and close it. Place the jar on top of a plate or other heatproof surface.

5. Light the candle (black and white are both good colors for protection) and pour the hot wax on top of the lid to seal it. Be careful not to burn yourself!

6. Keep this jar on your altar, if you have one, or anywhere in your house where you need extra protection.

Another creative way to use tea in your witchcraft is to use the loose tea leaves for spell jars. What's a spell jar? It is simply a jar filled with herbs, spices, and other ingredients that is meant to manifest your intent. It is then closed with a lid and sealed with hot wax. You can keep it in your altar, if you have one, or put it wherever you'd like in your home.

For a protection spell jar, white tea or matcha will work great. For a self-love spell jar, prioritize cherry, Earl Grey, or hibiscus tea. If you don't have loose tea leaves, you can just open a tea bag and pour the contents into the jar.

— JASMINE TEA MONEY BOWL —
FOR ATTRACTING MONEY

INGREDIENTS
....

A BOWL (any bowl will do, but you could pick a green one to symbolize wealth)

COINS or paper money

CINNAMON STICKS, for prosperity (ground cinnamon works, too, but might be messier)

JASMINE TEA (tea bags or loose tea leaves), to attract money

BAY LEAVES, for success

ANYTHING THAT REMINDS YOU OF MONEY, such as trinkets, anything gold or silver, glitter, crystals, or anything that you personally associate with wealth

A PIECE OF PAPER

A PEN, PREFERABLY GREEN (BUT BLACK WORKS TOO)

A GREEN CANDLE, for money (but you can also use a white candle)

1. Start by cleansing the bowl with water or incense smoke. If you use water, dry the bowl thoroughly.

2. Add the coins or paper money and the cinnamon sticks to the bowl. Add the jasmine tea, either in tea bag or sprinkled loose into the bowl. Add as many bay leaves as you'd like, but I like to add four to strengthen the spell. The number four is associated with the Emperor card in the tarot, which is sometimes referred to as "the provider," but you can pick any number that resonates with you. Add any other objects you've gathered for the spell to the bowl.

3. On a piece of paper, write your intent. Do you want money for a special project? Do you want to earn money from a new job? Write it down. Then fold the piece of paper and add it to the bowl.

4. Light the candle and keep it next to the money bowl. You should let the candle burn on its own (but of course keep an eye on it).

5. Interact with your money bowl every week: take or add money, augment it with symbolic new prosperity items, and light a new candle when you can.

There are different ways to prepare a money bowl, and each money bowl should reflect the person making it. This is the spell I personally use. You can add in any ingredients that make sense to you. For example, if you're trying to attract money through your art, you can add a paint tube. You can also add your business card, or anything that calls to you.

5

reading the
LEAVES

TASSEOMANCY, ALSO KNOWN as tasseography or tea leaf reading, is a complex divination method. "Tasse" comes from the French word for cup, and the suffix "-mancy" comes from the ancient Greek and means divination. In short, it's the art of divination in a cup.

So, how does tasseomancy work? Essentially, you read the dregs, or bits of liquid and tea leaves, in the bottom of your cup, interpreting the shapes to identify symbols that can convey a variety of meanings. This divination method is usually done with loose tea leaves used without a strainer, but it can also be done with coffee or wine dregs.

People have always tried to find what the future holds, and divination is an ancient practice. As for the history of tasseomancy, it is of course deeply entwined with the history of tea. While the origins of this divination practice are uncertain, many believe that it originated in China, ancient Greece, and the Middle East. As tea leaf reading was probably an oral tradition for a long time, there aren't many written sources to exactly pinpoint its provenance. However, the reading of coffee dregs can be linked back to the Ottoman Empire in the 1500s.

As for tea leaf reading as we know it today, it followed the trade routes of tea and is thought to have begun in the seventeenth century, when tea made its way to Britain through China. It started as an expensive beverage mostly reserved for the elite, but as trade led to falling tea prices, it became more accessible to the lower classes in England. At that point, tasseomancy became popularized. Using tea leaves for divination was much more convenient than the other methods used in Britain in the past, like molten wax and metal or animal entrails. The practice continued to grow in popularity in the eighteenth century when the nomadic travels of the Romani people helped spread tasseomancy all over Europe. In fact, the oldest book written in English about tasseomancy, *Reading Tea Leaves* by "a Highland Seer," dates back to the eighteenth century. But it's during the Victorian era, a time when people were particularly fascinated in the occult, that tea leaf reading became really popular.

There are many things to take into consideration when doing tasseomancy: the symbols themselves carry meaning, and their placement within the cup does as well. For instance, a bird means good news, but when it appears at the bottom of the cup, it is an indication that this luck will come in the distant future. In this chapter, I will present some of the symbols of tasseomancy that occur most often, the different placements inside the cup, and a step-by-step process that will guide you through reading tea leaves on your own with visual examples.

This chapter will give you some pointers and first tips to try it at home; use it as a springboard to explore tasseomancy in depth. There are many books and articles on the subject. After all, tasseomancy is a complex practice, and it might take you some time to master it.

I believe that divination should be used as a guide more than anything else, a way to peek into the future and find advice there. It's a great tool for self-development and introspection, as it connects us more deeply to our subconscious. If your tea leaf reading reveals bad news, remember to take it with a grain of salt and don't worry too much. Divination can give you valuable advice, and sometimes even a warning, but your actions alone define your future.

tea leaf reading symbols

When you finish drinking a cup of tea, you may have noticed the dregs left behind. If you take the time to study them, you'll see that these tiny bits of tea leaves left behind after steeping form certain shapes. Identifying the images they form and their meanings is the art of reading tea leaves. You can divide the symbols into four categories: animals, objects, letters, and numbers. Animals are usually tied to their culturally accepted symbolisms; for instance, a dog represents loyalty and a good friend. Objects are also often self-explanatory: a bed means rest and the sun represents happiness. Letters are generally thought to represent someone with that initial, and numbers are the indication of time. To read a teacup, however, you must read all the different symbols together and gather meaning from the entire composition.

Keep in mind that there are many different symbols, and the interpretations can differ depending on placement. This list isn't exhaustive, but it should give you a good overview of the different shapes and their meanings.

ANCHOR: luck and stability

ANGEL: good news

APPLE: success, especially in studies or career

ARCH: a journey abroad

ARROWS: if the arrow points down, bad news; if the arrow points up, good news

AX: difficulties and the overcoming of difficulties

BAT: futile journeys or tasks

BEAR: travels, usually for a long period of time

BIRD: good news and new journeys

BOAT: visit from a friend, protection

BOOK: if open, good news; if closed, hidden secrets

BOTTLE: temptation

BOUQUET: a very lucky symbol, usually tied to friendship, success, or love

BULL: slander, defamation

BUTTERFLY: success and pleasure

CAMEL: patience

CANDLE: enlightenment, help from others

CAR: visit from a friend

CASTLE: unexpected fortune, legacy

CAT: treason, difficulties, gossip

CIRCLE: success and completion, money

CLOUDS: usually indicates trouble, especially if the cloud is surrounded by dots (rain)

CLOVER: a very lucky symbol, happiness, prosperity

COFFIN: prolonged sickness, loss

CROSS: troubles, suffering or a blockage

CROWN: success, honor

DAGGER (OR SWORD): danger from self or others

DOG: loyalty, good friend

DOOR: opportunities

ELEPHANT: luck, longevity

EYE: be cautious

FIRE: if on top of the cup, achievements; at the bottom of the cup, danger

FISH: good news relating to money or family

FLOWERS: good fortune, success, happy love life

GOAT: stubbornness, the presence of enemies

GUN: anger, discord, danger where it points

HAMMER: hard work, overcoming challenges

HAND: if open, friendly help; if closed, an argument

HAT: success

HEART: good news, love, romance, meetings

HORSESHOE: good luck, good fortune

HOURGLASS: looming danger, upcoming decision

HOUSE: security, safety, success

HUMAN FIGURES: symbolism depends on what they are doing, but they are generally a good sign

KEY: understanding, prosperity

KNIFE: fighting, argument, strained relationships

LADDER: travel, evolution

LINES: if straight, a calm journey, progress; if wavy, an uncertain and challenging journey

MOON: a change in plan, success; if crescent moon, prosperity

MOUNTAIN: great goals, difficulties

NEEDLE: recognition

PIG: greed, carelessness, jealousy

PIPE: reconciliation, friendship

QUESTION MARK: uncertainty, curiosity, doubt, disappointment

RABBIT: bravery, success

ROSE: popularity, love, romance

SHELL: good news

SHOE: hard work, a change for the better

SNAKE: bad omen, caution

SPIDER: good luck, rewards

SQUARE: comfort, peace

STAR: health, hope, success

SUN: happiness, joy, power, success

TREE: luck, prosperity, happiness

TRIANGLE: something unexpected, good luck

TURTLE: slow progress

UMBRELLA: a period of difficulty, protection from troubles

WHEEL: if whole, good fortune; if broken, bad omen

Of course, no one expects you to memorize all the symbols! You can go back to this list anytime you need to, and you can also rely on your intuition when analyzing the dregs at the bottom of your cup. Sometimes a symbol can have different meanings depending on the culture, too. Don't hesitate to dig deep and look into a symbol, especially if a reading doesn't resonate with you. For that reason, you may want to get your hands on a dictionary of symbols.

THE TWELVE MONTHS
OF THE YEAR

This map of the cup is very straightforward, dividing it in twelve segments starting from the cup handle. Depending on the segment where your symbol is placed, you can tell if your reading will happen in the near future or not. If your symbol is on the seventh segment, it means that your prediction will happen in seven months.

PAST, PRESENT, FUTURE

This map is more complicated, but it also gives you temporal information about your reading. Here the cup is divided in circles and segments, going from the bottom of the cup to the rim. Each section represents the past, the present, or the future. Because it's more detailed, it will give you a clearer indication of time.

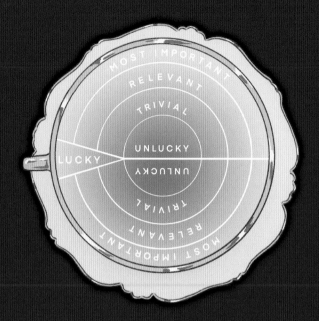

RELATIVE IMPORTANCE

Similar to the "past, present, future" map, this division of the cup is made of circles and segments. This time, however, it gives you an indication of importance. The closer to the bottom the symbol is, the more trivial the message. Meanwhile, a message near the rim is very important.

the different maps of the cup

Identifying the symbols is only half of the process. When reading tea leaves, the interpretation is essential. And to help you interpret the message of the leaves, you must pay close attention to the placement of the symbols.

Think of the cup as a map. Depending on where the symbol is placed, your reading can be very different. There are various ways to read that map. Placement can affect the level of importance of a message, the temporality of a message, or even its meaning. For example, a symbol on the rim of the cup usually symbolizes a good omen, while its appearance at the bottom of the cup can symbolize bad news.

Here are some ways to divide your cup.

The concentration and distribution of the tea leaves in the cup can also give you some information about your reading. For instance, if the dregs overall look balanced and harmonious, it can indicate stability. A very dense cup can be a sign of focus, even obsession. Meanwhile, scattered dregs can indicate stress or a loss of focus.

Tasseomancy is an *intuitive* method of divination. There are many ways to read tea leaves, and a reading is always open to interpretation. Because what you see in the cup depends on your perception, it is important to be in tune with your instincts. If something doesn't make sense, you might have to think of a different map for your placements, or even look at a symbol dictionary to try to find another meaning that might click more with your intuition. You can also try rotating your cup to find different perspectives.

how to read tea leaves

Now that you know everything about symbolism and placement, it's time
to read your first cup of tea. Follow the process step by step and go for it!
Remember that divination is a practice, and like everything else, it might
take you a while to really master it. Take your time, and have fun.

You will need:

- ❧ **A WHITE CUP (OR A LIGHT-COLORED CUP) WITH A
  NARROW BOTTOM AND A WIDE RIM.** No need to invest in
  a tasseomancy cup, although they do exist. A teacup you already
  own will be just fine, although you shouldn't use a mug or a dark-
  colored cup, as it will impact the reading. A mug doesn't have
  angled sides, and you need them so the tea leaves can cling to the
  cup. Dark-colored cups will make it a lot harder for you to discern
  the dregs, so avoid them, particularly when you begin doing
  readings.

- ❧ **LOOSE TEA LEAVES.** Because you need your tea to actually
  form dregs in the bottom of the cup, you can't use tea bags for
  tasseomancy. If you don't have loose tea leaves, you can open
  a teabag and use its contents, but keep in mind that the leaves
  might be too fine for divination. In fact, the bigger the leaves, the
  better! However, you can choose any tea you like: black, white,
  herbal—it doesn't make a difference. If you want, you can pick

teas that enhance relaxation and meditation like oolong, or lavender, sage, or fennel tea.

Once you have tea and a cup, it's time to start. First, you'll want to make sure the conditions are right. Set up in a place with a peaceful, relaxing atmosphere. That might mean lighting some incense or candles, or playing some white noise or calming music. You might feel nervous at first, and that's okay! I know that I can get a little bit restless before a divination session. What helps me is to breathe deeply and light some incense, but we all have our own ways to relax. You can even meditate first to ground you more deeply within yourself.

If you're doing a reading for someone else, make sure they are comfortable too. Divination will generate conversations and questions, so everything needs to be cozy during *and* after the reading. If you're reading for yourself, it's a good idea to prepare some nice things you can rely on afterward, like a warm blanket or a snack you really love. Divination is a deep dive into our subconscious, and it can be draining.

ADD THE LOOSE TEA LEAVES AND HOT WATER TO A TEAPOT. Do not use a strainer; instead, put the tea leaves directly into the water. You can pour the tea immediately or let it steep for a bit. When reading your own fortune, you can brew the tea leaves directly in the cup. But if you are reading someone else's fortune, it's best to use a teapot first.

ASK A SPECIFIC QUESTION IF YOU LIKE. If you are wondering about what the future holds and you have a question, now is the time to ask! While your tea is steeping, ask the question out loud or focus on it. The more specific, the better. You can ask anything you like. Do you want to know if you'll get that promotion at work? Or if you're going to buy the house you really want? Express your question clearly and meditate on it. If you are reading someone else's fortune, they should ask their question out loud, and both of you need to focus on their question while the tea is brewing.

POUR THE TEA INTO A CUP. If you're reading someone else's fortune, pour the tea into their cup. If you're reading your own fortune, pour it into your cup. The person getting the reading should be the one drinking the tea. Allow the leaves to fall into the cup with the tea.

DRINK THE TEA UNTIL THERE IS ONLY A LITTLE BIT OF LIQ-UID LEFT IN THE BOTTOM OF THE CUP. There should still be just enough liquid to ensure the tea leaves will stay in the bottom after you drink.

SWIRL THE DREGS IN THE CUP. Swirl it slowly clockwise three times to ensure that the leaves are evenly distributed and not stacked in the bottom of the cup. (Three is a magical and auspicious number with deep spiritual connections.) If you prefer, you can also turn your cup upside down onto a saucer before turning it upright again.

START BY GOING WITH YOUR FIRST IMPRESSION. Take a first glance at the shapes. What do you see? What shapes do you recognize? What kinds of emotions do they evoke in you?

NOW, YOU CAN START ANALYZING THE TEA LEAVES, TAKING INTO ACCOUNT THE SYMBOLISM AND THE PLACEMENTS OF

THE SHAPES. The handle is thought to represent whoever is getting the reading, which means that it should be your starting point. From there, read the rest of the cup in a clockwise direction.

The symbols need to relate to you (or whoever is getting the reading), so trust your instincts. If something doesn't feel right, then it might not be right! This isn't a science: tasseomancy is open to interpretation. The most important thing is to have fun with it. Don't put pressure on yourself, and don't see divination as a determining practice. Always remember that *you're* in charge of your destiny.

sample readings

It can seem daunting to apply theory to practice when it comes to tasseomancy. There are many elements to take into consideration, and when confronted with the actual dregs at the bottom of your cup, the sight can be disarming. Hopefully these visual examples will better help you understand how to decipher the different symbols and make your own readings.

These examples are, of course, fictional and aren't meant to read your future. They are just tools to show you how you can apply the different symbols and cup divisions into a reading.

Readings can be subjective, and you might find similar symbols in your cup and yet come up with a different interpretation depending on the context, the question, or the person getting the reading. Trust your instincts, and remember to have fun with it!

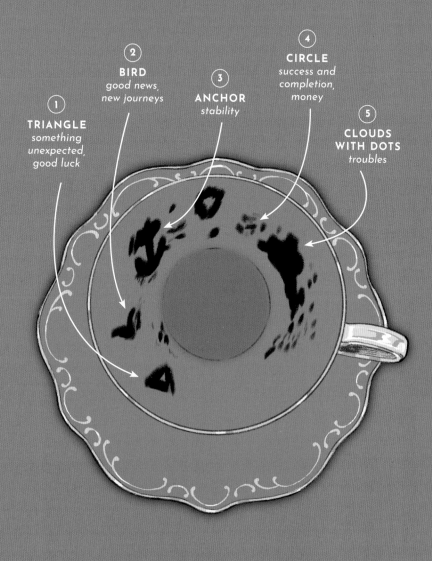

1. TRIANGLE
something unexpected, good luck

2. BIRD
good news, new journeys

3. ANCHOR
stability

4. CIRCLE
success and completion, money

5. CLOUDS WITH DOTS
troubles

READING #1

Starting the reading from the handle, the **TRIANGLE** (1) is symbolic of good luck. The handle represents the nearest future, meaning that something unexpected but positive is about to happen very soon. The **BIRD** (2) is a sign of good news and new journeys, which emphasizes that this new, unexpected event will bring positive changes to your life. As we move clockwise and away from the handle, the **ANCHOR** (3) symbolizes stability. This stability should occur in a couple of months, and even later lead to success with the **CIRCLE** (4). The circle is close to the rim, which can indicate that you should focus on the success this new journey will bring you. While there are some **CLOUDS** (5) in your future, which are a sign of troubles, these clouds are close to the bottom of the cup, which could mean that these troubles will be trivial and you shouldn't pay them too much attention, lest you risk forgetting about your blessings.

The overall message of this reading is that you are at a crossroad, and this new journey you are embarking on will lead to success and stability. While changes often bring their fair share of discomfort and troubles, remember to focus on the positive.

And, of course, always adapt the meaning of a reading to fit the situation. While here I am keeping things vague, this reading could work for money or work issues, romance, or even family problems.

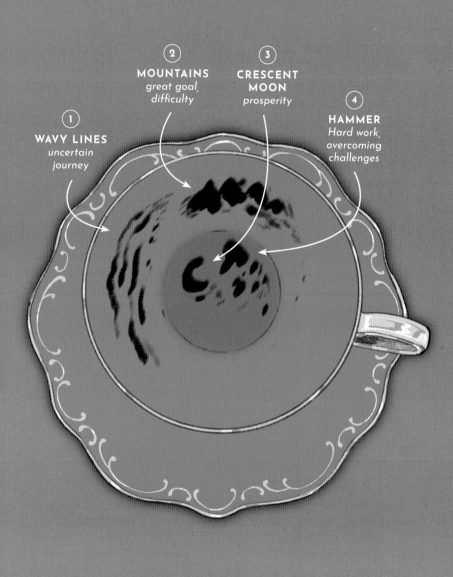

① **WAVY LINES**
uncertain journey

② **MOUNTAINS**
great goal, difficulty

③ **CRESCENT MOON**
prosperity

④ **HAMMER**
Hard work, overcoming challenges

READING #2

Just like with the other example, we start the reading with the handle, going clockwise. The first recognizable symbols are the **WAVY LINES** (1), which go around a good chunk of the cup. Wavy lines indicate the presence of an uncertain journey in your near future. If we cut the cup into segments representing months, we can see that this will stretch for a few months, maybe up to four or five months. This journey will not be an easy one, as shown by the presence of **MOUNTAINS** (2) in the dregs; however, they also symbolize the accomplishment of a great goal. The **CRESCENT MOON** (3) is placed at the bottom of the cup, which can mean that prosperity lies in your distant future. Added to the symbolism of the **HAMMER** (4) next to it, we can conclude that it is through hard work, and by overcoming the challenges met during your journey, that you will eventually be successful and prosperous.

To simplify and connect all the elements together, this reading means that a long period of hardships and hard work might be needed for you to achieve your goals and succeed. This journey and challenges could be work related or connected to some relationship problems being eventually fixed. Again, remember that the reading must make sense in relation to the context and situation. If this reading was meant to answer a specific question, adapt the meaning to fit this question.

next steps

You now have all the basics to start your journey with tasseomancy. It is a highly personal and intuitive divination practice, so remember to listen to your instincts. You can dive deeper into tea leaf reading by reading books, watching videos, and, of course, practicing readings for yourself and your loved ones.

Always keep in mind that divination is not deterministic. Whatever future is predicted in your cup, whether it be good or bad, is yours and yours alone to make or break. Your actions and your decisions always pave the way for the trajectory of your life. So while the tea leaves can give you advice, messages, and sometimes even warnings, they don't write your destiny for you. Only you can do that.

CONCLUSION

There is something in the nature of tea that leads us into a world of quiet contemplation of life.

—LIN YUTANG, *THE IMPORTANCE OF LIVING*

Now that you are on your way to understanding and practicing tea witch-craft, I hope that this book gave you some insight into all the power a sim-ple cup can hold and, by extension, the power that you already possess. Whether you are a beginner, a seasoned witch, or simply someone who really loves tea, you can now brew some magic at home and watch as the universe reacts to the energy you have poured into it—puns intended.

Tea is already a warm, comforting beverage. What could be more perfect for catalyzing your goals and intentions? The act of making yourself a cup of tea has, in a way, always been a ritual: picking a nice cup and the right tea to match your mood, pouring the hot water, waiting patiently for the tea to steep and the water to cool down, and finally, the warm satisfaction of drinking the beverage you have prepared for yourself. Or perhaps a loved one made that cup for you, and this ritual was imbued with all the care and affection they have for you. Tea isn't a drink you can rush. It needs time to settle in the water and infuse it with taste. It is an invitation to mindfulness; it is a time you make for yourself to simply enjoy something soothing. From there, it is really just a small step to witchcraft.

After all, witchcraft consists of rituals: preparing a spell, celebrating nature, and finding magic in the simple acts of everyday life. This is the heart of magic.

Everyone has their own practice and perception of witchcraft, of course, and thus this book can only reflect my own experiences and the knowledge I have accumulated as best as I could over the years. Learning and teaching have always been an essential part of my art, and I firmly believe that knowledge is never meant to be kept to oneself. My work has consistently been connected to the desire to explain and share what I know, while accepting that I will always have so much more to learn. What a beautiful thing to accept!

I remember when I started to create my first book of shadows in a little black notebook, feeling lost and overwhelmed by all the things I had to understand and discover, and finding help from people who were so open about what they knew and what they had already learned. So, if you have found some help in these pages, I will consider myself quite lucky.

I have kept this same black notebook by my side while writing this book, as a reminder that just like I was helped in my journey, it is quite humbling to be able to now share with others what I have learned.

And at the risk of repeating myself, don't get discouraged if a spell doesn't work right away or if your tea leaf reading just isn't clicking. Learning is a beautiful process that is bound to involve some bumps in the road. Witchcraft, like any other craft, requires practice and patience. If you're like me and can be a little bit of a perfectionist, you know that it can actually seem quite daunting. It sounds nice, in theory, to be great at everything from the start. But failure is a part of learning—it is in fact the most important part! And if we knew everything from the start, life would surely be very boring. The act of learning itself requires that we first face what we do not know.

Tea magic is a love letter to yourself. It is the act of taking something simple and yet so comforting and using it as a tool to help yourself navigate life and all the obstacles you might face. So, always remember to be kind and gentle to yourself, to be just as soothing as a cup of tea can be.

2

ACKNOWLEDGMENTS

As an illustrator and an avid reader, writing a book such as this one was always a huge dream of mine. And how incredible and exciting to be given this amazing opportunity! I want to thank Union Square & Co. for entrusting me with this project. And a special thanks to my amazing editor, Kate Zimmermann, for helping this book take shape with patience and dedication.

I am so grateful to my partner, Yacine, for always giving me honest, genuine feedback, even when I get really sensitive about it (oops—sorry about that). You kept me grounded when anxiety was trying to take the wheel, and you always reminded me of my own strength. Day after day, you help me grow and you always believe in me, especially when I don't believe in myself. I feel very blessed to have you by my side.

To my mom, who is my self-proclaimed biggest fan and my own personal medium, thank you. Having an artist for a mother is a lucky thing in itself when you're an illustrator, but I am even luckier to always have your love, your support, and your trust.

I also want to thank my friends for helping and supporting me throughout this entire adventure, even from afar and while sometimes living in totally different countries. And I want to give Lisa, Rachel, and Cara a special thanks for agreeing to taste test my tea spells and giving me feedback so I could make sure these spells were the tastiest they could be.

And finally, I am forever grateful to all the people who follow my journey on Instagram. I know social media can sometimes be a complicated place, and yet I am lucky enough that my followers have always been the kindest, most uplifting community an artist could ever dream of. I am always so excited to share my art with all of you, and it truly feels like being among friends. I wouldn't be here today if it wasn't for this community. Thank you.

ABOUT THE AUTHOR

CHLOÉ ZARKA GRINSNIR is a freelance illustrator. She loves witchcraft and fashion, and she incorporates these things into her illustrations. She is obsessed with historical fashion, cottagecore, pretty dresses, and fall aesthetics. Instagram: @chloe.z.arts